Venus and Serena Williams

by Jonatha A. Brown

Reading consultant: Susan Nations, M.Ed., author/literacy coach/consultant

WR WEEKLY READER

EARLY LEARNING LIBRARY

Please visit our web site at: www.earlyliteracy.cc
For a free color catalog describing Weekly Reader® Early Learning Library's list
of high-quality books, call 1-877-445-5824 (USA) or 1-800-387-3178 (Canada).
Weekly Reader® Early Learning Library's fax: (414) 336-0164.

Library of Congress Cataloging-in-Publication Data

Brown, Jonatha A.
   Venus and Serena Williams / by Jonatha A. Brown.
     p. cm. — (People we should know)
   Includes bibliographical references and index.
   ISBN 0-8368-4470-X (lib. bdg.)
   ISBN 0-8368-4477-7 (softcover)
   1. Williams, Venus, 1980-—Juvenile literature. 2. Williams, Serena, 1981-—United States—Juvenile
literature. 3. Tennis players—United States—Biography—Juvenile literature. 4. African American women
tennis players—Biography—Juvenile literature. I. Title. II. Series.
   GV994.A1B76   2005
   796.342'092'2—dc22
   [B]   2004058757

This edition first published in 2005 by
Weekly Reader® Early Learning Library
330 West Olive Street, Suite 100
Milwaukee, WI 53212 USA

Based on *Venus and Serena Williams* (Trailblazers of the Modern World series) by James Buckley Jr.
Editor: JoAnn Early Macken
Designer: Scott M. Krall
Picture researcher: Diane Laska-Swanke

Photo credits: Cover, title, pp. 6, 10, 12, 14, 16, 17, 19, 20, 21 © AP/Wide World Photos;
pp. 5, 8 © Al Messerschmidt/WireImage.com; p. 7 © Ken Levine/Getty Images

Printed in the United States of America

1 2 3 4 5 6 7 8 9 09 08 07 06 05

Table of Contents

Words that appear in the glossary are printed in **boldface**
type the first time they occur in the text.

Chapter 1: Little Girls

Venus Williams was born on June 17, 1980. Her sister Serena is younger. She was born on September 26, 1981. They have three older sisters.

Both girls grew up to be rich and famous, but they once were poor. They grew up near Los Angeles, California. They lived in a bad neighborhood. It was not a safe place for kids.

Hoping for a Chance

Their father wanted a better life for his girls. He wanted them to live in a nice house and play in safe places. But he did not earn much money. He could not afford a better home.

Mr. Williams liked to watch **professional** tennis on TV. He saw that some of the players won a great deal of money. That gave him an idea. He would teach the girls

Mr. Williams has coached and cheered for his daughters for many years.

to play tennis. He thought they might be good at it. If they were, maybe they could play professionally. Then they might get rich. The family could move to a nicer area.

He began to teach the girls to play. At first, it seemed that his idea would not work. The three older girls did not like tennis. But Venus and Serena loved it. Before they were five years old, they could hit a ball back and forth. This was pretty good for such young kids!

Their father became their coach. He spent many hours teaching them to play, and they kept coming back for

more. When they started school, they could not play as often. Their parents made them put school first. So they both studied hard and got good grades. They still played tennis when they could. They were becoming good players.

The girls began to enter **tournaments**. At most of these events, they were the only black players. All the other kids were white. Some of them did not want to play against black kids. But Venus and Serena kept playing, and they usually won.

In 1991, their family moved to Florida. The girls started working with Rick Macci, a **famous** tennis coach.

Rick Macci coached Venus (shown here) and Serena for more than three years.

Chapter 2: Turning Pro

Venus and Serena went to school for half of the day. Then they played tennis with their new coach for the other half of the day. Both girls worked hard. Their playing got better and better.

Fourteen-year-old Venus was excited about turning pro.

Venus and Serena worked with Mr. Macci for three years. For a short time, they worked with another coach. Then their father said they were ready to turn **pro**. They were both about fourteen years old at the time. Most people thought this was too young. They said Mr. Williams was pushing the girls too hard. But he was sure it was a smart move.

The First Pro Years

Venus played in her first pro **match** in 1994. Her sister turned pro a year later. They did not play in many matches at first. Both girls started out slowly, and they still put school first.

They did not win in their first few years as pros. Still, they played well and kept getting better. Tennis fans liked watching them play. The girls were becoming well known.

In 1995, the Reebok Corporation made a deal with Venus. They paid her to wear their clothes on the court. Venus got a lot of money. This deal was just what her father had hoped for. For him, it was a dream come true. Money was no longer a worry.

Serena was seventeen years old when she won her first Grand Slam event — the U.S. Open.

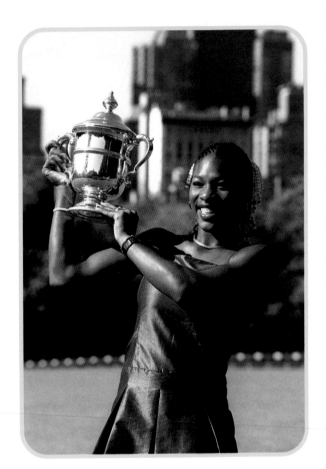

For Venus, it was also a dream come true — and she was only fifteen years old! The family moved to a mansion. The sisters had their own tennis court.

Venus and Serena entered more tournaments in 1997. They played singles —

two people against each other. They also played doubles. In doubles tennis, two people play on each team. The girls played both games well, but they did not win.

Then came the U.S. Open. This is a Grand Slam tennis event. There are four Grand Slam events. They are the U.S. Open, the French Open, the Australian Open, and Wimbledon. These are the most famous tennis events in the world.

Reaching for the Top

Both girls entered the 1997 U.S. Open. Venus won match after match and made it to the finals. There she played Martina Hingis — the top player in the world. Venus lost that match, but her family was proud of her. They had good reason to be proud. Venus was the second black woman ever to reach

As the girls grew older and stronger, they began to win doubles tournaments.

the finals in the U.S. Open! She was making history!

This great day also had an ugly side. Some players said Venus had been rude to them. Her father said that was not true. He said he had heard other players speak rudely to Venus. He said they had **insulted** her because she was black.

These angry words pointed out a problem — some of the other players did not like the sisters. In part, they did not like them because they were different. Their skin was dark. They wore beads in their hair. They dressed in wild clothes. They also spent more time together than with the other girls. Some players thought Venus and Serena should not dress or act that way. They thought the two black girls should try to fit in with the white girls.

Being Themselves

Venus and Serena did not agree. They did not want to change, and they did not see why they should. They ignored all the talk, and they did not change. Instead, they kept dressing and acting as they liked.

Chapter 3: Winning

Venus began to win in 1998. That year, she won three events. Serena did not win, but she played some fine games.

The 1999 Lipton Championship was very exciting. Both girls won their early matches. Then they had to face each other in the finals. It was sister against

The 1999 Lipton Championship gave fans a thrill. They watched as the sisters played against each other in the final match.

sister, and their fans loved it! At the time, Venus was a stronger player. Few people were surprised when she won.

That year, Venus went to the U.S. Open with high hopes. Yet she did not play her best, and the tournament did not go well for her. It was her sister's turn to shine. Serena played well. She made it to the finals. There she faced Martina Hingis. Martina had beaten Venus two years earlier. Serena won in a close match. It was her first big win in singles tennis!

Time to Heal

The next year did not go smoothly. Both girls were hurt. Venus hurt her wrist, and Serena hurt her leg. They had to take time off to heal.

Venus and Serena were back in shape for Wimbledon. They won their early matches. Then they played each other. Venus was still stronger, and she beat her sister. Then she went on to win in the finals. She was the first black woman to win Wimbledon in many years.

Arthur Ashe was a very skilled black player. He won three Grand Slam events.

Next, Venus won the U.S. Open. Then she played in the Olympics and won two gold medals. In the end, the year 2000 was a great one for her. She did so well that *Sports Illustrated for Women* named her Athlete of the Year!

Serena also played in the Olympics. She and Venus won the gold medal in doubles. They were both great players. But when they played against each other, Venus usually won. She could hit balls so hard that Serena could not hit them back.

Venus was not the only player who stood in Serena's way. Jennifer Capriati could beat her, too. In fact, she beat Serena three times in 2001. Serena was only twenty years old, though. She had not yet reached her peak. She kept working at her game. She kept getting stronger and playing smarter.

Venus lunges for the ball and slams it over the net.

Chapter 4: On Top of the World

In 2002, Serena's hard work began to pay off. She began to beat both Venus and Jennifer! The first time was in Florida. The next was at the French Open. That year, Serena won three Grand Slam titles in a row. She was coming on strong.

Sisters, Rivals, Friends

Venus and Serena are **rivals** on the court, but they are still best friends. They share a home. They room together when they are on the road. They cheer for each other at matches and celebrate each other's wins. They do not let the tennis net come between them.

Venus also had a great year. In February, the World Tennis Association (WTA) ranked her number one. It was a big moment. She was the first black player ever to rank first! Serena was not far behind. In fact, she was ranked number two. For the first time in any major sport, two sisters were on top!

Venus beat Serena to win the U.S. Open in 2001. She won that event two years in a row.

The girls were overjoyed to win the gold medal in doubles tennis at the 2000 Olympics.

Their standings changed in 2003. Serena won two Grand Slam titles that year. Then she ranked first in the world. Venus was number two.

That year, Venus got hurt. She strained a muscle and could not play until it healed. Then she hurt her right leg in early 2004. This meant more time off. Venus was not alone. Serena was also hurt in 2003. She had to stop playing for a while, too. But she began playing again the next year.

No one knows how long the two will play. Whatever the future brings, however, a few things are certain. First, they will be rich, just as their father hoped. Also, they will long be remembered for their big wins.

Venus and Serena do not always wear tennis outfits. Here they show off lovely gowns at an important dinner.

Glossary

famous — well known

insulted — said mean things

match — a game or contest

professional (pro) — playing a sport for money

rivals — people who play against each other

tournaments — contests

For More Information

Books

Serena and Venus Williams. Mary Hill (Children's Press)

Tennis. My Favorite Sport (series). Jonatha A. Brown (Weekly
   Reader Early Learning Library)

Venus and Serena Williams. Discover the Life of a Sports Star
   (series). David Armentrout (Rourke)

Web Sites

Venus and Serena Williams

www.sportsline.com/u/kids/women/williams_sisters.htm
A biography on the Kids' Zone Women's History Month Web site

Venus Williams Pictures

*yahooligans.yahoo.com/Sports_and_Recreation/Tennis/Players/
   Williams__Venus/Venus_Williams_Pictures/*
A few great shots of Venus

Index

About the Author

Jonatha A. Brown has written several books for children. She lives in Phoenix, Arizona, with her husband and two dogs. If you happen to come by when she isn't at home working on a book, she's probably out riding or visiting with one of her horses. She may be gone for quite a while, so you'd better come back later.